Strategic Studies Institute
and
U.S. Army War College Press

THE RESURGENCE OF AL-QAEDA IN SYRIA AND IRAQ

Azeem Ibrahim

May 2014

*****

Comments pertaining to this report are invited and should be forwarded to: Director, Strategic Studies Institute and U.S. Army War College Press, U.S. Army War College, 47 Ashburn Drive, Carlisle, PA 17013-5010.

*****

*****

The Strategic Studies Institute and U.S. Army War College Press publishes a monthly email newsletter to update the national security community on the research of our analysts, recent and forthcoming publications, and upcoming conferences sponsored by the Institute. Each newsletter also provides a strategic commentary by one of our research analysts. If you are interested in receiving this newsletter, please subscribe on the SSI website at *www.StrategicStudiesInstitute.army.mil/newsletter.*

FOREWORD

By 2010, it was possible to see al-Qaeda as an organization in decline. It had lost militarily in Iraq and seemed politically irrelevant to the popular revolts during the Arab Spring. However, the Syrian civil war has allowed it to rebuild and, in the form of the local Al Nusrah Front, use a revised political and military strategy. This important monograph considers if these apparent gains can be sustained or whether al-Qaeda's ideology will again alienate other salafist groups and the wider Sunni population.

Dr. Azeem Ibrahim bases his report on available evidence, interviews, and visits to Syria. At the moment, the Assad government seems to be making some gains, and the rebel forces are split into three broad groups of the Free Syrian Army, the Islamic Front (backed by the Gulf States), and two al-Qaeda groups (Al Nusrah and the Islamic State in Iraq and Syria [ISIS]). ISIS has alienated all the other factions and is likely to retreat to Iraq, but the Al Nusrah Front is operating in a loose alliance with the Islamic Front. What is not clear is if Al Nusrah's approach of seeking to cooperate with other Islamist groups and of trying to build popular support will allow it to make the substantial territorial gains that al-Qaeda has been seeking since it fled Afghanistan.

Dr. Ibrahim argues that this attempt is likely to fail. Even though Al Nusrah has shown a willingness to cooperate with the Islamic Front, the latter is likely to have to reject any long-term alliance with Al Nusrah if it wishes to retain funding from the Saudis and the Gulf States. In itself, ensuring that al-Qaeda remains marginalized will do little to help Syrians suffering the 4th year of civil war, nor will it eliminate the risk

v

of radicalized foreign fighters returning to their home countries. However, it does suggest that al-Qaeda's relative resurgence since 2010 will be limited, and the organization as a whole will be no closer to its desire to reestablish territorial control over a large region where it can operate with relative safety.

The Strategic Studies Institute offers this monograph for consideration in the ongoing discussion regarding al-Qaeda and the organizations affiliated with it.

DOUGLAS C. LOVELACE, JR.
Director
Strategic Studies Institute and
   U.S. Army War College Press

ABOUT THE AUTHOR

AZEEM IBRAHIM served as a Research Fellow at the International Security Program of the Kennedy School of Government at Harvard, a World Fellow at Yale, Fellow and Member of the Board of Directors at the Institute for Social Policy Understanding, and an Adjunct Research Professor at the Strategic Studies Institute, U.S. Army War College. He has met and advised a number of world leaders and governments on a diverse range of issues ranging from financial investment, to geopolitics, to countering extremism. He served as a reservist in the United Kingdom's 4th Battalion Parachute Regiment. Dr. Ibrahim holds a Ph.D. from the University of Cambridge.

SUMMARY

The Syrian civil war has allowed al-Qaeda to recover from its setbacks up to 2010. Its main affiliate in the region seems to be testing a new strategy of collaboration with other salafist-jihadist groups and a less brutal implementation of Sharia law in areas its controls. In combination, this might allow the Al Nusrah Front to carve out the sort of territorial control of a region (or state) that al-Qaeda has sought ever since its eviction from Afghanistan.

On the other hand, Syria has also seen a civil war between two al-Qaeda inspired factions (Al Nusrah and the Iraq-based Islamic State in Iraq and Syria) and there are indications of limits to al-Qaeda's ability to cooperate with other anti-Assad factions and gain popular appeal.

The extent that the Syrian civil war offers the means for al-Qaeda to recover from its earlier defeats will determine whether the organization has a future, or if it will become simply an ideology and label adopted by various Islamist movements fighting their own separate struggles.

THE RESURGENCE OF AL-QAEDA IN SYRIA AND IRAQ

INTRODUCTION

The purpose of this monograph is to review the current resurgence of al-Qaeda (AQ) in Iraq and Syria. Al-Qaeda affiliates now occupy more territory in the Arab world than at any time in its history. However, this resurgence may be a temporary phenomenon, with al-Qaeda taking advantage of the chaos in Syria, the weak government response in Iraq, and the simmering discontent in other Muslim countries that has followed the Arab Spring. Their recent gains are substantial, but there are reasons to doubt if al-Qaeda's power and appeal within the wider salafi-jihadist movement, especially in Syria, can be sustained. Here, different coalitions have recently disavowed al-Qaeda and, in some cases, are in open conflict with its militias. There is a case to argue that al-Qaeda has managed to exploit an opportunity but lacks the ability to broaden its appeal sufficiently to make long-term gains.

This report is based on an extensive analysis of current national security reports and interviews with global experts; the author recently traveled to Turkey and Syria to interview individuals knowledgeable about al-Qaeda. A definitive assessment of the significance of al-Qaeda's resurgence in 2013 remains inconclusive, as 2014 brings further turmoil, conflicting information, and shifts and changes with new alliances, leaders being killed or replaced, and territory won and lost.

One conclusion that is emerging, however, is that the imposition on civilian communities of extreme fundamentalist Sharia law is not welcome or accept-

1

able anywhere, especially if al-Qaeda continues with its violent and brutal suppression of other political currents within radical Islam. While their goals may be similar, the so-called "moderate" salafi-jihadists seem to have a better appreciation of how to win over the wider population than al-Qaeda.

Despite the attention paid to the resurgence of al-Qaeda, the bigger problem dominating the Middle East scene is the escalation of the Sunni-Shia divide. This split is reflected in the civil wars in Syria and Iraq and, in turn, has an international aspect as Shia Iran and Sunni Saudi Arabia are fighting a proxy Muslim civil war, particularly in Syria.

It may turn out that al-Qaeda is just one of the many pawns in this tragic and explosive situation, and that its resurgence will last only as long as the money and power behind the conflict continues in a war where it increasingly seems that no one can win. However, the clear warning from Syria is that al-Qaeda has the capacity to exploit any unrest to its own ends, even if it fails to then take control of the situation.

BACKGROUND

A common narrative from the U.S. administration has been to proclaim the final demise of al-Qaeda. In reality, it is still not clear if "we are winning or losing the war on terror."[1] Despite the United States spending an estimated $5 trillion[2] on the war on terrorism, (including veterans' costs and interest on borrowing the funds), al-Qaeda has managed to reconsolidate itself very quickly in Iraq and Syria. This may be due partly to the failure of U.S. policy in dealing with the crisis in Syria. However, it indicates that al-Qaeda has the capacity to exploit new opportunities. It has learned from experience and is more organized, better funded, more media and public relations aware, and more dangerous than ever before.

The failures of Western intervention in Afghanistan, where, in spite of all that has been attempted, the situation is fragile, and Iraq, increasingly racked by sectarian violence, provides one way in which al-Qaeda can recover. Add to this, the relative failure of the democratic opportunities offered by the events of the Arab Spring after 2010[3] in Egypt, Libya, and Tunisia means all those states are now facing domestic terrorism and sectarian violence. In addition, the gradual shift in Syria from popular revolt to outright civil war has created the scope for al-Qaeda to extend its reach from northern Iraq and threaten to dominate the opposition to the Assad regime.

One interpretation is that al-Qaeda has recovered from its losses in the period up to 2010 and has managed to emerge as a dominant force and ideology across the Islamic world, taking advantage of political upheaval and Western failures. However, while al-Qaeda, in its most recent manifestation in Iraq and Syria, appears to be alive and well, what is not clear is how much of the current structure is the old pre-September 11, 2001 (9/11) al-Qaeda, and how much is a new organization using the label of al-Qaeda. This has led to genuine confusion about exactly what al-Qaeda is today, and if it is still a hierarchical organization with a leader or a more amorphous ideology which people freely adopt and interpret as a brand name and set up "franchises" relevant to their national situation. If the apparent resurgence is to be understood, then paying careful attention to what is, sometimes lazily, labeled al-Qaeda is important.

Political, economic, or religious differences in Muslim countries have created violent opposition to the existing dictatorships, whether Western-backed or not, and they all tend to be called "al-Qaeda" when they should really be seen as either the various regional affiliates of official al-Qaeda or the more pervasive form of salafi-jihadism. Every religious terrorist is not necessarily a member of al-Qaeda, and al-Qaeda does not represent all groups within the global salafi-jihadist movement. These differences are becoming increasingly apparent in Syria as the civil war rages on and fluid alliances are continually being made and broken within the opposition to the Assad regime. Jihadism in Syria is revealing the fault lines between al-Qaeda and other Sunni freedom fighters and may give us a better indication of whether al-Qaeda is surviving, transforming, or slowly dying.

To survive, al-Qaeda needs leadership, funding, and territory in which to operate. This territory needs to be within the chaos of failing or transitional states, where al-Qaeda can operate outside the law of the land, thriving in a civil vacuum. At the moment, Syria is the obvious temporary home for al-Qaeda, where it can operate with impunity. However, its inability to co-opt all the other jihadi factions in the country indicates that there are significant limits to its power and influence.

In the Syrian war setting, al-Qaeda followers are primarily fighters rather than ideologues, and their loyalties are to their immediate brothers in arms and leaders in the field. However, these leaders in turn swear an oath of fealty or "bayat" to Ayman al-Zawahiri, who, since the death of Osama bin Laden, has been in hiding, probably in Pakistan's Northwest Frontier, the birthplace and the stronghold of not only al-Qaeda, but the global militant-Islamist movement and the Taliban. The same can be said for al-Zawahiri that was said about Osama bin Laden:

> how to respond to an enemy who is a man and not a state; who has no structured organization, no headquarters, and no fixed address; and whose followers live in different countries and feel a loyalty not so much to that man as to the ideology of militant Islam.[4]

The war in Syria is becoming "a quagmire of sectarian violence"[5] as the revolutionary opposition has been splintered by rival militias turning on each other instead of uniting against the Assad regime.

The leading al-Qaeda faction, the Al Nusrah Front, is losing credibility among fellow Muslims who do not agree with their mission and have refused allegiance to al-Qaeda leaders. The other former al-Qaeda militia (Islamic State in Iraq and Syria [ISIS]) has already been discredited and rejected by other rebel coalitions. News from Syria in November 2013 blames the recent advances by Assad forces on rebel in-fighting, according to the British-based Syrian Observatory for Human Rights. This in-fighting is partly a struggle for control over arms and resources but also reflects a rejection of the hard line approach to social issues of the two al-Qaeda factions in the country. It is also a matter of ideology and a struggle for funding from the Gulf States among the Islamist and salafi-jihadist militias.

In the short term, the remaining al-Qaeda contingents in Syria are more concerned with establishing an Islamic state than defeating Assad's forces. Equally, the newly formed Islamic Front is seen as a move to attract funding from the Gulf, to the further exclusion of al-Qaeda factions, including the Al Nusrah Front. Some more enlightened Al Nusrah leaders have responded to this threat by trying to moderate their policies to win hearts and minds, and their success or failure will indicate the ability of al-Qaeda to endure or whether its hard-line fundamentalism finally renders it irrelevant, unable to appeal to a wide enough strata of society to allow it to take real control over a state or region.

AL-QAEDA SINCE 9/11

In his July 18, 2013, testimony to the House Committee on Foreign Affairs Subcommittee on Terrorism, Nonproliferation, and Trade, Thomas Joscelyn defined al-Qaeda as:

> a global international terrorist network, with a general command in Afghanistan and Pakistan and affiliates in several countries. Together, they form a robust network that, despite setbacks, contests for territory abroad and still poses a threat to U.S. interests both overseas and at home.[6]

This is hardly a description of a dying organization.

On the other hand, according to White House transcripts, President Barack Obama has described al-Qaeda as having been "decimated," "on the path to defeat," or some other variation of these phrases, at least 32 times since the September 11, 2012, attack on the U.S. consulate in Benghazi, Libya.[7] He has since had to limit his statement to the Taliban in Pakistan and al-Qaeda affiliates in Yemen, whose leadership has been decimated by drone attacks. Variously dismissed as "a bunch of guys in caves"[8] or "a ragtag group of jihadists,"[9] some commentators seek to dismiss al-Qaeda members today as thugs or criminals, a localized but containable problem like the Mafia in the 1940s or the Assassins of the 12th century.

Other counterterrorism analysts suggested that the killing of Osama bin Laden had defeated al-Qaeda, along with the impact of the successful drone strikes in Pakistan's tribal regions, which have killed 38 al-Qaeda and Taliban leaders.[10] Some claim that al-Qaeda was already on the decline before 9/11, and that that one grand atrocity was its last major accomplishment. An alternative to this is that, as Jacob Shapiro suggests, the 9/11 attacks were only possible because al-Qaeda had the secure space in Afghanistan to operate, organize, and create a hierarchical system to train and motivate terrorist operatives.

> When terrorist groups have a great deal of operative space and can build large, relatively formalized organizations, they can indeed be quite deadly. Terrorist groups, of course, can no longer operate in that manner without attracting a great deal of lethal attention from various governments and it is hard to imagine such permissiveness will be allowed any time in the near future.[11]

In effect, there is a strong argument that either al-Qaeda managed one spectacular strike due to luck, or to the extent to which it was embedded in secure bases in Afghanistan. Since then, it has lost its secure base, most of its original leadership, and has been in strategic retreat over the past decade. However, just 1 year after the Benghazi attack in 2012, al-Qaeda has been described as transformed, reconstituted, or rebuilt, and Syria has become key to this resurgence. In effect, it is no longer "on the run" but has managed significant gains and, for the first time since it was evicted from Afghanistan, has a substantial region under its direct control. We are thus faced with a confusing interpretation of the relative strength of al-Qaeda and its capacity for future actions.

One argument is that the mostly successful counterterrorism actions since 9/11 have meant that al-Qaeda has never since been able to carry out a similar crime with the same impact and terrible loss of life. Seventeen Americans have lost their lives to terrorism since 9/11, and some consider this as defeat for al-Qaeda. For example, Thomas Lynch in a New America Foundation debate on October 17, 2012,[12] argued that al-Qaeda has been defeated, reasoning that apart from the death of its charismatic leader, Osama Bin Laden, it has failed to achieve its stated objectives, it has achieved nothing since 2006, and importantly, it has failed to co-opt salafi-jihadists to its ranks. Conversely, other analysts cite the proliferation of terrorist attacks all over the world as evidence that al-Qaeda is still functional in that it has successfully inspired other jihadi movements. They argue that although Osama Bin Laden is dead, the al-Qaeda movement lives on as "a network, not a hierarchy," and its resilience and adaptability allow it to flourish as localized affiliates in many countries around the world.

For example, Bruce Reidel, director of the Intelligence Project at the Brookings Institution, wrote on September 27, 2013:

> The horrible attack on a shopping mall in Kenya this week, the attack on a natural gas plant in Algeria earlier this year and the ongoing growth of al-Qaeda franchises in Syria all underscore the remarkable ability of al-Qaeda and associated movements to attract volunteers from across the Islamic world to its ranks. Al-Qaeda has achieved a long-sought goal of Islamist politics: the creation of a pan-Islamist militancy that operates across national borders and national politics. This transnational quality is one of the keys to al-Qaeda's remarkable regenerative capacity, its ability

to survive massive counterterrorism campaigns and rebuild operational capability quickly.[13]

This points to a major problem in understanding al-Qaeda. As one writer put it, "Al Qaeda is a lot of things. It's partly an ideology, it's partly a political-cultural force, and it is also a state of mind."[14] This has led to a degree of fragmentation, especially since Ayman al-Zawahiri took over, following the death of Osama bin Laden in 2011. The al-Qaeda inspired groups that have become established in many parts of the world do not necessarily take orders from al-Zawahiri, nor are they funded directly by him.

This implies there are a substantial number of salafi-jihadists groups that are not part of al-Qaeda, and there are many degrees of influence, inspiration, and affiliation. Thus, only those groups which have sworn allegiance to al-Zawahiri should legitimately be called al-Qaeda. Beyond these few groups, there is simply a more amorphous network of al-Qaeda sympathizers, subscribing to the al-Qaeda mythology and using the name when it is to their advantage.

One way to understand this nexus of groups is to see al-Qaeda as:

> far from being a fly-by-night, fragmented terror organization, Al Qaeda is attempting to behave like a multinational corporation, with what amounts to a company-wide financial policy across its different chapters.[15]

Thomas Joscelyn's testimony to a Congressional committee in July 2013 described al-Qaeda as a strong organization:

The backbone of today's al Qaeda consists of its 'general command' in Afghanistan and Pakistan (others refer to this as the 'AQ Core') and its formal affiliates. The established al Qaeda affiliates include: Al Qaeda in the Arabian Peninsula (AQAP), Al Qaeda in Iraq (AQI) and the Islamic State of Iraq (ISI), Al Qaeda in the Islamic Maghreb (AQIM), and Shabaab in Somalia. All of the affiliates have publicly sworn bayat (an oath of fealty) to al-Qaeda's senior leadership. Jabhat al Nusra in Syria should also be included in this list as well, because the group has openly proclaimed its allegiance to Ayman al-Zawahiri.[16]

This distinction is made by other commentators, such as former National Security Agency and Central Intelligence Agency Director Michael V. Hayden, during an appearance on CBS on December 29, 2013, who stated that the al-Qaeda movement is divided into three layers: "al-Qaeda prime, formally affiliated and like-minded." General Hayden told *The Washington Times* on December 30, 2013, that there are still uncertainties about who precisely executed and ordered the attack on Benghazi, but that he could say with confidence that the perpetrators were "al Qaeda affiliated if al Qaeda is viewed as a movement, a cause, a concept."

This is giving the organization a very bureaucratic aspect. "They have to have bookkeeping techniques because of the nature of the business they are in," said Brookings Institution fellow William McCants, a former adviser to the U.S. State Department's Office of the Coordinator for Counterterrorism. "They have so few ways to keep control of their operatives, to rein them in, and make them do what they are supposed to do. They have to run it like a business."

The picture that emerges is of a rigid bureaucracy, with a chief executive, a board of directors and departments such as human resources and public relations. Experts say that each branch of the terror group replicates the same corporate structure, and that this strict blueprint has helped al-Qaida not just to endure but also to spread.[17]

At the same time, many of the franchises are operating independently, and it is difficult to establish which of the jihadist groups are still loyal to the "old" al-Qaeda and which have broken away to pursue their own actions, independent of funding or even direction from al-Qaeda leadership. Joscelyn describes them as being outside the formal affiliates but describes them as "ideological kinsmen":

We often cannot see the operational ties between these groups because al Qaeda still maintains a substantial clandestine apparatus that is tasked with hiding such relationships. For some of these organizations, there may very well be no concrete ties and their relationship al-Qaeda's jihad is purely rhetorical.[18]

The controversy about those responsible for the attack on the U.S. Embassy in Benghazi in 2012 is one example of the confusion surrounding the name of al-Qaeda. At the time it was often described as an "al-Qaeda" attack, but *The New York Times* published an article on December 29, 2013,[19] stating that, according to their extensive interviews with Libyan militants, the perpetrators of the attack were not al-Qaeda. Guy Taylor of the *Washington Times* had a somewhat different analysis:

Counterterrorism analysts and former high-level officials indicated during interviews with *The Washington*

Times last summer said that the FBI [Federal Bureau of Investigation], which was tasked by the Obama administration with carrying out an investigation into the attack, had settled on a broad conclusion: The attack was carried out by a combination of militants with varying degrees of connection to three Islamist groups: Ansar al-Sharia, the uhammad Jamal network, and Al Qaeda in the Islamic Maghreb.[20]

This pattern is also emerging in Syria. Here, there are different factions of salafi-jihadist fighting forces, and the divide between the mainstream Syrian opposition and the extremist jihadi groups is creating a war on several fronts with a very volatile situation of allegiances that are constantly shifting and changing. With the hard-line al-Qaeda faction (ISIS) now denounced by several alliances of jihadist militias, al-Qaeda's resurgence in Syria has suffered a definite setback, with implications yet to be revealed. Al-Qaeda's remaining "official" militia in Syria is now the Al Nusrah Front. In combination with the return of al-Qaeda in Iraq in the Anbar province, recent events in Syria indicate that gaining territorial control is an important goal, but that al-Qaeda is having problems imposing its will on other salafi-jihadist groups.

One issue is that al-Zawahiri, like Osama bin Laden, lacks combat experience but does not have the charisma or authority of al-Qaeda's former leader. He remains in hiding and in early September 2008, the Pakistan Army claimed that they had "almost" captured him after getting information that he and his wife were in northwest Pakistan. Currently, the U.S. Department of State is offering a reward of U.S.$25 million for information about his location.

Al-Zawahiri to date has been unable to match the organization and funding achieved by Bin Laden, and his contact with his followers is constrained by his existence as a fugitive. In the videos released at intervals to rally his followers, he shows he is aware of the need for a better public image. Bin Laden himself in some of his later writings acknowledged that al-Qaeda ("base" in Arabic) was no longer a good brand name as he was failing to attract funding and followers due to general revulsion against his violent and self-defeating agenda.[21]

However, al-Zawahiri is still totally committed to his vision of a global caliphate as he explained in his 2001 autobiography, *Knights Under the Banner of the Prophet,* that the most important strategic goal of al-Qaeda was to seize control of a state, or part of a state, somewhere in the Muslim world, explaining that, "without achieving this goal, our actions will mean nothing." In this sense, the struggle to control large areas of Syria and northern Iraq are clearly critical to al-Qaeda being able to carry out its overall goals.

In October 2013, Ayman al-Zawahiri delivered a recorded audio speech on the occasion of the 9/11 attacks, revealing according to Al Arabiya, that he "has begun to suffer from frustration and incapability of activating al-Qaeda's strengths." The most important point of the speech was that America will remain "the first target of al-Qaeda members' operations" as per the strategy of individual jihad—which is the only means left for the organization.[22]

Al-Zawahiri, from his refuge in Pakistan, has belatedly realized that the militants' increasing ferocity and widespread practice of *takfir* (declaring other Muslims infidels) is not winning over the Muslim world.[23] His authority has obviously been undermined by events in Syria and the defection of ISIS. This may mean his attention seems to have shifted instead to Pakistan rather than Syria. As reported in the Pakistan newspaper, *Dawn,* on September 19, 2013, he urged fighters to "create a safe haven for Mujahideen in Pakistan" so that it can become a base for "establishing an Islamic system."[24] As William McCants says, "Zawahiri's inability to manage al-Qaeda's sprawling organization offers a preview of the infighting to come after his inevitable death."[25]

THE WIDER DYNAMICS OF
JIHADI TERRORISM

Jihadi terrorism has been in existence for a long time, with attacks preceding the formation of al-Qaeda, and not all the resurgent salafi-jihadis in Syria choose to call themselves part of al-Qaeda nor wish to swear allegiance to al-Zawahiri. Despite its claims, al-Qaeda is not aiming to unite all Muslims, as it is strictly Sunni and violently anti-Shia. In addition, it is not able to gain the loyalty of either all Sunni traditions or even of all Sunni militant groups.

In effect, to understand some of the dynamics in Syria means understanding the logic and goals of the various groups opposed to the Assad regime. This is difficult, as "there is a natural tendency to shy away from treating terrorists as rational actors."[26] In particular, there are some differences of opinion as to the main motivating force of the salafi-jiahdists, with some analysts suggesting that funding, food, and guns are more powerful than ideology. "Size, money, and momentum are the things to look for in Syrian insurgent politics — ideology comes fourth, if even that."[27]

However, others such as Professor Joshua Landis, believe that ideology rules.[28] The public statements by the various militia leaders are an indication of their commitment to the cause of first defeating the Assad regime, and then establishing an Islamic state. In this respect, it is now possible to discern two major strands. One is of groups aligned with al-Qaeda, such as the Al Nusrah Front and ISIS, and the other are the newly formed Islamic Alliance, which is a further consolidation of the merger of two major ideological streams within the Syrian rebels — the moderate Islamists and the salafists.

The Alliance rejects secularism, which it defines as dividing religion from life and society, and is developing its own political bureaus and platforms in an effort to challenge those of the Syrian National Coalition. While civilian populations have demonstrated their opposition to ultra-radical influences, they are becoming more supportive of groups that advocate the implementation of some form of Sharia law in the country.[29]

> The Islamic Alliance stated on Nov. 26 that it wants to replace Syria's regime with an Islamic state, but insisted it would protect minorities and not create an 'oppressive, authoritarian system'. However, they did not provide a clear vision of a post-Assad Syria, perhaps fearing that going into details would splinter the alliance of seven key Islamist groups which hopes to unify the fractured opposition.

> The Islamic Front says representative government 'is based on the notion that the people have the right through institutions to (determine) legislation, whereas in Islam God is the sovereign'. But it adds: 'This does not mean that we want an oppressive, authoritarian system', saying Syria should be ruled through a Shura, or Islamic consultative council. The new coalition includes a Kurdish Islamic faction, and also says it rejects 'any project to partition' Syria.[30]

Syriacomment.com provides up-to-the-minute information about the fluid nature of the insurgency, noting that "powerful leaders are emerging and smaller militias are lining up with the larger sharks."[31] The opposition remains extremely fragmented and volatile, but salafi-leaning insurgents are the single most dominant force in liberated areas. These groups may not represent even half of the insurgency but are major actors in their areas.

While ISIS and the Al Nusrah Front attract media attention because of their al-Qaeda affiliation, past or still existing, the other fighting factions in Syria deserve attention regarding their ideology and makeup as "moderate" forces, possible counterweights to al-Qaeda. The Syrian Islamic Front is the biggest alliance of salafi-jihadis, and, while many would like to see them as "moderate," they are committed first to defeating Assad's troops and then to creating an Islamic state, as opposed to al-Qaeda which is committed first and foremost to global jihad.

Aron Lund's recent comprehensive reporting for *Syria in Crisis*[32] notes that the Islamic Front wants "to establish an independent state where God's merciful law is sovereign and where the individuals of this state enjoy justice and a dignified life." It spurns the term "civil state" (*dawla madaniya*) as misleading and rejects democracy and parliamentary rule. They appear to be envisioning "a republican theocracy supervised by religious scholars where there is some degree of political competition within sharia-compliant but otherwise modern institutions and where the role of politicians is to administer a strict application of sharia rather than to make laws of their own."

The militias who make up the Islamic Front now outnumber the Free Syrian Army (FSA). As the new coalition excludes the two al-Qaeda groups, the Al Nusrah Front and ISIS, some would like to see it as a more moderate coalition that is marginalizing the truly radical factions.[33] The jihadi culture has adapted with the times, and the fiercely independent Islamic Front is now seen to have three main objectives: to further isolate ISIS now that it has created its own downfall; to encourage the Al Nusrah Front to become more mainstream; and to create a viable rebel army with clear command and control.[34]

In contrast, an insight into al-Qaeda's motives and strength in Syria was provided by the analyst Cole Bunzel in his February 2013 translation of a document posted on Shumukh al-Islam, al-Qaeda's premier online forum. Purporting to be a "comprehensive strategy" for the Al Nusrah Front in the ongoing Syrian jihad representing the forum membership's thinking as a whole, the document is particularly revealing in two respects:

> First, contrary to the triumphalist tone of much Syrian jihadi media, the Shumukh members are not upbeat in their description of ongoing and anticipated events. For the present, there is hope mixed with desperation and fear; for the future, a strong sense that the jihadis will suffer strangulation from all sides. In their worldview, some form of Western intervention to stymie jihadi success is all but assured; the West, with its Israeli and Iranian allies, will seal Syria's borders and proceed to eliminate the jihadi threat, carving up Syria and elevating the 'Islamists' to power.

> Second, Shumukh's recommendations presuppose a very long war in Syria. These include such things as rapidly increasing the number of recruits before the borders are sealed, making sure to take control of the regime's heavy and unconventional weapons, estab-

lishing a unified media organization for more effective propaganda, and refraining, at all costs, from allying with 'Islamists' such as the Muslim Brotherhood, no matter how attractive this might seem.[35]

The Al Nusrah Front (Jahbat al-Nusrah) is directly subordinate to al-Qaeda leader Ayman al-Zawahiri. The rival ISIS, led by Abu Bakr al-Baghdadi, despite its resurgence in Iraq, is being run as a renegade operation since al-Baghdadi defied al-Zawahiri's leadership. These two al-Qaeda branches have an estimated 6,000-7,000 operatives,[36] and new recruits are continuing to arrive in large numbers. The other salafist rebel groups in Syria total about 100,000;[37] thus the proportion of fighters with formal al-Qaeda loyalty is comparatively small. There are many groups who are on record as disavowing al-Qaeda, but that adhere to the salafi-jihadi objectives, adding to the complexity of predicting the strength of al-Qaeda as a distinct ideology, network, and organization.

This would support the view that al-Qaeda is divided effectively from other jihadist groups in Syria. Thus, not only is it at war with the regime and those who follow the Shia traditions, but is also at variance to other radical Sunni groups. In addition, even those who directly share its ideology are split into two factions. This may indicate that there are limits to its ability to influence events. However, in combination with its resurgence in Iraq, it is clear that al-Qaeda is again a major force.

AL-QAEDA'S RESURGENCE IN IRAQ

Al-Qaeda's resurgence in Syria was preceded by its recovery in Iraq, where it was "dead on its feet" in 2010 and has rebounded strongly since then. A successful relaunch of the movement in April 2011 led to a significant recovery of territory within Iraq's Sunni communities, notably in the Anbar province, making the country less stable and cohesive, and effectively merging its struggle in Iraq with the Syrian civil war.

> The Syrian crisis is strengthening Al Qaeda in Iraq and Iraqi militants are in turn, complicating Syria's future path. Operating as the Islamic State of Iraq and al-Shams (ISIS) Al Qaeda in Iraq has ambitions to dominate the Salafi terrorist scene in Syria.[38]

Since 2011, the Shia dominated government in Baghdad has alienated Iraqi Sunnis by discrimination and repression, with the result that many Sunnis have moved to the Anbar province, making it an al-Qaeda stronghold on the border with Syria.

The Institute for the Study of War, in an October 9, 2013, report, assessed that al-Qaeda in Iraq (AQI) has reconstituted as a military force:

> Al-Qaeda in Iraq is resurgent. Al-Qaeda in Iraq (AQI) reached its apex of territorial control and destructive capability in late 2006 and early 2007, before the Surge and the Awakening removed the organization from its safe havens in and around Baghdad. Subsequent operations pursued AQI northward through Diyala, Salah ad-Din, and Mosul, degrading the organization over the course of 2007-2008 such that only a fraction of its leaders, functional cells, and terroristic capabilities remained and were concentrated in Mosul. As of August 2013, AQI has regrouped, regained capabilities, and expanded into areas from which it was expelled during the Surge.[39]

Control of terrain is important to AQI, as it thrives in a chaotic environment from which it may emerge as the most well-organized contender. AQI seeks to create this disorderly condition as it pursues control of urban terrain presently secured by the forces of the Iraqi State.[40]

The AQI stated aim is to gain control of Mosul to destroy popular confidence in the Iraq administration; to isolate Mosul's population and government from the state; to exploit the ethnic and social fractures within Mosul's diverse community; to intimidate the population into tolerance of AQI's presence; and then later to compete with local and provincial governance structures for control. However, the brutality of AQI is appalling, with civilian casualties of more than 5,500 since April, 2013, according to United Nations (UN) figures. As of August 2013, AQI has increased the frequency and volume of bombing attacks and has also carried out attacks upon critical infrastructure, such as the Um Qasr port at Basra.

> The United States has reacted by reaffirming the $10 million bounty placed on Abu Bakr al-Baghdadi, the leader of AQI, whom officials said was based in Syria in August 2013. Targeting AQI's leader, however, will not be effective in halting the organization's growth. AQI is no longer a small cadre based around a single leader, but rather an effective reconstituted military organization operating in Iraq and Syria.[41]

Much of the renewed violence has been attributed to foreign jihadists who come into Iraq from Syria, creating one large conflict zone, which has also spilled over into the Lebanon.[42] The situation in Iraq at the beginning of 2014 has become increasingly violent. Al-Qaeda Islamic State in Iraq and the Levant (ISIL) militias seized Fallujah on January 2, 2014, and have attacked Ramadi, seeking to consolidate their hold on the Anbar province on the border with Syria. The Iraqi

Army and the local tribes are fighting back. Ahmed Abu Risha, head of the Awakening National Council—a coalition of tribesmen in Anbar—said "there is an open war against ISIL," with the tribes forming a bloc against the al-Qaeda group with the help of local police.

However, the extent of this counterstroke by the government is in doubt. A report in Al Arabiya on January 3, 2014, reiterates that:

> Baghdad's failure to recruit the awakening movement's fighters into the formal army and the exacerbation of the conflict in Syria have encouraged al-Qaeda to reemerge in the strategically important Anbar province that connects Iraq to Syria, Jordan and Saudi Arabia.[43]

Michael Knight's December report to Congress states that, although al-Qaeda in Iraq has been a fairly insular terrorist group for many years:

> Al-Qaeda's resurgence in Iraq is undeniably damaging to US interests in Iraq, in the broader regions and potentially in the homeland security environments in Europe and the United States.[44]

AQI has been self-funding since 2010 through organized crime such as kidnap for ransom; protection payments from large Iraqi companies; plus trucking, smuggling, and real estate portfolios. However, the organization may be in danger of overreaching, as Sunni Arabs and tribesmen become resentful of al-Qaeda as it becomes more powerful. This is culminating in the recent escalation of conflict in Fallujah and Ramadi where tribal forces and the Iraqi Army were under attack by al-Qaeda militants.

ISIS has now gained a territorial chain of control stretching from Ramadi, 100 kilometers (km) west of Baghdad, to Al-Raqqah in northern Syria, 160-km from Aleppo. Commander Abu Bakr al-Baghdadi vows to establish an Islamist caliphate, presenting a direct threat to Israel, Jordan, Saudi Arabia, and Lebanon. Despite these successes, ISIS has been disowned by al-Zawahiri and the formal al-Qaeda leadership. In effect, particularly in Syria, there are two groups that share al-Qaeda's ideology but are at war with each other.

AL-QAEDA IN SYRIA — ISIS AND THE AL NUSRAH FRONT

While the civil war is still being waged in Syria and it becomes increasingly dangerous for journalists, it is difficult to get reliable, detailed information about the al-Qaeda organizations operating alongside the rebel opposition.

> The rival sides (the supporters and opponents of the regime) customarily issue biased and manipulative reports whose sole purpose is to further their own interests. Each side claims to be winning and each side slanders the other. Another difficulty is the nature of the Al Nusrah Front and the Islamic State in Iraq and Greater Syria (ISIS). They are both closed decentralized organizations with many rivals and which are careful to preserve their secrecy, and do not reveal, even to their own operatives, information about their leaders or about how they operate.[45]

To understand the situation, it is necessary to consider ISIS and Al Nusrah as separate organizations, even if they essentially share the same ideology.

ISIS.

In April 2013, AQI declared itself the ISIS, expanding its historical identity to include Syria. Its leader, Al-Baghdadi, had played a key role in establishing the Al Nusrah Front and considered Abu Mohammed al-Golani, Al Nusrah's leader, to be his subordinate with a duty to obey him.

Baghdadi attempted to integrate Jabhat al-Nusrah (the Al Nusrah Front) into ISIS, with the new organization being called the Islamic State in Iraq and al-Sham, ISIS. ISIS took control of wide areas without much resistance, benefitting from the Jabhat al-Nusrah fighters who defected to ISIS.[46] Al-Baghdadi claims descent from the Prophet Muhammad and has been described as a "philosopher jihadi," something quite different from other al-Qaeda leaders.[47] His leadership ambitions and his brutal methods of enforcing Sharia law have alienated ISIS from the populace and the Syrian Islamic Front.

ISIS is estimated to have about 8,000 soldiers in both Syria and Iraq, who were recruited without checking the quality of the new members. ISIS started paying $200 a month for each fighter, and thousands of men in ISIS's area of control joined the group. Al-Baghdadi continues to be openly defiant of al-Zawahiri's directives and, according to a jihadist source quoted by the Iranian news source Alalam:

> Baghdadi believes in the necessity of declaring the emirate, or Islamic state, immediately and declaring its emir as its leader who alone [makes decisions], and for the mujahedeen to swear allegiance to that Islamic state in the territories [it controls], be they Syrian or non-Syrian, and by not recognizing the Sharia com-

mittee judges who come from other Islamic factions. There should be no law but ISIS's law. Also, all Islamic factions should swear allegiance to the ISIS emir or be considered outside of God's authority. Military cooperation happens only with the battalions that declare exclusive allegiance [to ISIS]. And ISIS preachers (mosque preachers) have the right to replace the local preachers in all mosques. Moreover, all the spoils and financial resources belong to the ISIS's treasury. The other factions, whether or not they are Islamic, have no right to that money.[48]

ISIS has been criticized for attacking fellow rebels and establishing its own fiefdom. It fought against the FSA, for example, in Azaz, north of Aleppo, so that it could take control of the border crossing with Turkey to capture revenue and control goods moving to Aleppo. Turkey closed the border crossing in response.[49] ISIS also sought to establish a foothold in the northeast section of Syria that borders Iraq. However, this is being contested not only by Assad's forces, but by Syrian Kurds who are taking advantage of the unrest by planning to form a transitional administration. Iranian Fars News reports on November 27, 2013, that Syrian Kurdish fighters have intensified their attacks against ISIS and recently seized the sole border post at Yarubiya held since March by al-Qaeda-linked groups on their border with Iraq.[50]

By adding the Kurds to their list of enemies, ISIS would seem to have too many enemies to be able to survive for long. Instead of concentrating on defeating the Syrian Army, it has taken over two towns from the FSA forces and seems to be intent on establishing a foothold for an Islamic state, creating in Syria's north a series of fiefdoms run by rival warlords. This self-serving aggressiveness, along with its brutality, has led, among others, to American al-Qaeda spokesman Adam Gadhan recommending that al-Qaeda publicly sever its ties with the Islamic State of Iraq because its sectarian violence tarnished AQ's reputation.[51]

Al-Zawahiri, in a broadcast on Al Jazeera TV on November 9, 2013, declared that Golani's Al Nusrah Front would continue to function as "an independent branch of Al Qaeda that reports to the general command." He said that al-Baghdadi had "made a mistake by establishing the [ISIS] without asking for our permission." "The Islamic State in Iraq and the Levant is to be abolished while the Islamic State of Iraq remains functioning," al-Zawahiri said.[52] Subsequently, al-Qaeda has stressed that it:

> has no connection with the group called the ISIS, as it was not informed or consulted about its establishment. It was not pleased with it and thus ordered its suspension. Therefore, it is not affiliated with al-Qaeda and has no organisational relationship with it. . . . Al-Qaeda is not responsible for ISIS's actions.[53]

On October 5, 2013, Cole Bunzel of *jihadica.com* noted that ISIS persisted "in a state of outright disobedience to its supposed seniors in Al Qaeda Central (AQC), Zawahiri among them."[54] Brookings Institution's William McCants said, "In the 25 year history of Al Qaeda, no affiliate has ever publicly disagreed with the boss so brazenly."[55]

Since the defection of ISIS, both al-Qaeda branches have entrenched themselves as independent organizations in the Syrian theater of operations. The split has been widely covered on jihadi forums and social networking websites, with some supporting the ISIS, some the Al Nusrah Front, and others both groups equally, for they each are waging jihad against the enemy. On the ground, however, the Al Nusrah Front is attempting to maintain its popular support among the Syrian people, whereas ISIS has initiated attacks on fellow Muslim rebels and has instituted draconian Islamic law in towns it controls. ISIS does not seem to have learned from experience in Iraq where al-Qaeda's brutal campaigns have alienated many Sunnis and led to its isolation. Since its takeover of the eastern city of Raqqa in May 2013, ISIS has focused on solidifying its rule through intimidation, creating an economy of dependence, and seeking to integrate eastern Syria with its strongholds in Iraq. Minorities have been hounded out of the city and foreign journalists and aid workers are no longer welcome; dozens are presently in ISIS captivity.[56]

According to Chris Looney, writing for *Syria Comment:*

> Its hostility towards minority groups, draconian legal system, and brutal repression of dissidents has generated a significant backlash, severely undermining the group's credibility and keeping it from being seen as a legitimate part of the opposition. Because of this, ISIS' current governance strategy is likely unsustainable.
>
> Still, ISIS thrives on instability, and as the Syrian war reaches its 1,000[th] day with no end in sight, the group is likely to be able to maintain its hold in Raqqa. Whether it can learn from its mistakes remains to be seen, but absent a dramatic shift in the trajectory of the conflict, ISIS is here to stay.[57]

That dramatic shift has now taken place, with ISIS rejected not only by the al-Qaeda leadership, but also the Al Nusrah Front and almost all the other rebel factions because of its uncompromising ideology and imposition of strict Sharia law on the areas it holds.

The Al Nusrah Front.

The Al Nusrah Front was designated by the United States as a Foreign Terrorist Organization in May 2013. According to a Quilliam Foundation report,[58] al-Qaeda sent operatives from Afghanistan to Syria as early as 2000 to train them for the fighting in Iraq. In March 2011 when the Syrian uprising began, AQI sent trained Syrian and Iraqi guerilla fighters back into Syria, where they later defined themselves as an autonomous organization and strengthened their direct links with al-Qaeda, formally becoming an al-Qaeda branch called Jahbat al-Nusrah (JN), or the Al Nusrah Front.

Many cadres of the Al Nusrah Front come from the jihadist network of Abu Musab al-Zarqawi, which was built during the 2000s and centered in Baghdad in 2002, following Al-Zarqawi's arrival from Afghanistan via Iran. Syrians who had been with Al-Zarqawi in Herat, Afghanistan, in 2000 were sent to build branches of his network in Syria and Lebanon, with Al-Zarqawi exercising control from Iraq. These jihadists established "guesthouses" in Syria to channel would-be fighters to Iraq and the infrastructure flourished. During this period, Syria acted as the main channel for funding for the network, with Saudi and Gulf Cooperation Council (GCC) jihadists in the Levant securing financial support from sympathisers in their home countries.

On January 24, 2012, the Al Nusrah Front was formally announced with the objective of establishing an Islamist state in Syria and a caliphate in Greater Syria, by its leader Muhammad al Golani (also spelled Al Julani). His name reflects the fact that he is probably from the Golan Heights, and is thought to have close ties to Abu Musab al-Zarqawi and AQI. A secretive figure, he has several times been pronounced killed in battle,[59] yet he appeared recently on Al Jazeera TV, his back to the camera, and his face covered by a black scarf.

Al-Golani has renounced the FSA, saying it was a crime to accept the aid of Western countries in the war to topple the Assad regime. He also announced his opposition to Turkey as a U.S. ally and opposes both the Arab League and Iran. By refusing to cooperate with the pro-democracy opposition, the Al Nusrah Front has fragmented the anti-Assad forces, a counterproductive stance as it is also alienating the international community.

The Al Nusrah Front is very selective about initiating new members, requiring *tezkiyya*, or personal assurance, from two commanders on the front line, stating that the recruit has the necessary skills, religious commitment, and attitude to join the group.[60] Recruits are tested in the field for courage and loyalty to the Front's ideology. According to the Quilliam Foundation report:

> This is part of the reason JN [the Al Nusrah Front] has been so successful—other rebel groups such as the Free Syrian Army (FSA) have a policy of mass recruitment which makes them appear strong, but actually leaves them chaotic and disunited.

Another Al Nusrah Front leader, Al-Amir Gazi al-Haj, said his group is effective because it has extremely high standards. "We only accept the best of the best," he is quoted in an interview.

> We have pure intentions. We fight only for Allah. We do not accept even small deviations [from God's law],

like smoking. We walk a straight line, and you can see the results.

> Al Nusrah Front's new recruits take an oath of allegiance or al-Bay'ah. The religious nature of this oath, swearing before God to follow the jihadist leadership, makes it a stronger, more personal contract than a simple civil oath would be. Breaking this oath carries significant danger, with jihadists in Algeria killed for refusing to follow the leaders to whom they had pledged allegiance. The religious basis of this oath means that recruits have no legal recourse should they wish to leave the group, as they have made a vow to submit to jihadist leaders entirely, unless their instructions go against the will of God.[61]

The exact number of foreigners is not known, but approximately 7-11 percent of the volunteers come from West European countries (mainly the United Kingdom [UK] and France) and Muslim countries in Central Asia (mainly Chechnya).[62] Their motivation and ideology differ — some are motivated by sectarian considerations, some by a hatred of the Assad regime, and some volunteer because of a sense of adventure and the heroic image of the rebels.

Many come to Syria to join the FSA but then transfer to the Al Nusrah Front because of better salaries and equipment, organization, and resources. Many adopt the salafi-jihadi ideology only after staying in Syria, where they undergo an accelerated process of radicalization. Concern exists in their home countries that when the operatives return, having undergone military training and radicalization, they will potentially engage in radical activity and terrorism. But as volunteering to fight Assad is not a crime in the volunteers' countries of origin, authorities have no effective way of dealing with the phenomenon.

While Syrians continue to suffer, sandwiched between a brutal dictatorship and extremist groups, Arab and European jihadists are being indoctrinated and trained in the world's most active battle zone—experience they may someday bring home.[63] The brigades are made up of thousands of volunteers from the Arab Muslim world, such as Libya, Tunisia, Saudi Arabia, and Egypt who now make up the majority of its members. The process of jihadist operatives joining the ranks of the Al Nusrah Front is still going on.[64]

While admitting to receiving help from the Iraq branch since the early days of the insurgency, Golani said that the Al Nusrah Front would continue operating under its own banner, with loyalty to al-Zawahiri. "The banner of the Front will remain the same, nothing will change about it even though we are proud of the banner of the (Islamic) State and of those who carry it," he said.[65]

The Al Nusrah Front leadership is aware of the negative publicity that is created by indiscriminate attacks killing civilians but are outspoken through their own media network, *al-Manara al-Bayda*, about the sectarian nature of their mission; revenge against al-Nusayrin (Alawites) for their mistreatment of ahl al-Sunna (Sunnis).

> Once the Ba'athist regime falls, JN's opponents will become many and varied. Moderates who support the group's strong stance against Assad may grow to be repulsed at the continuing violence and increasingly extreme rhetoric which could follow the fall of the regime.[66]

This has proved to be the case with the excesses of ISIS and, while Al Nusrah may be more pragmatic in its statements, it clearly represents a mortal threat to anyone from different confessional groups or who hope for a democratic, secular Syria. It remains to be seen whether the Al Nusrah Front has learned from the ISIS mistakes and will temper its rhetoric and actions in the field. The ability to make the transition from being a combat organization to gaining popular acceptance will be crucial in determining the limits to the current al-Qaeda resurgence.

AL-QAEDA AND POPULAR GOVERNANCE

Al-Qaeda's efforts at building community trust and respect among beleaguered citizens in war-torn Syria is an indication of whether it will be a movement that prevails, or whether it is simply a wartime phenomenon. Its record of nation-building internationally has been negligible, and recent events are proving that "significant grassroots hostility is building in liberated parts of Syria against foreign-funded extremists and al Qaeda affiliates."[67]

It would seem vital to al-Qaeda's survival to have the support of the local populace in whatever country it seeks to become established, otherwise it simply remains an organization that attracts deracinated young men, adventurers, malcontents, and religious zealots with a taste for violent adventure. Al-Qaeda has always been associated with violence and destruction, unlike the Muslim Brotherhood, which historically attempted to create community loyalty through public service. This is important, as Syria has a tradition of relative pluralism and tolerance:

> Syria has been a pluralistic secular society for decades. The majority of its Sunni Muslim population are conservative and have coexisted peacefully alongside the

many other religions and ethnic minorities that make up Syria's diverse society, history, and culture. The people of Syria do not aspire to a Saudi sponsored Salafi/Wahhabi leadership or doctrine of law.[68]

The Syrian people would appear to be reluctant participants in the attempt to establish an Islamic state. The actions of ISIS and the Al Nusrah Front in the areas they now control will be an indication of their future staying power based on their governance of the civilian populations. At present, the establishment of Sharia law and tribunals is the one unifying factor of the different rebel factions, and their imposition of Sharia law on civilians seems to be tolerated as long as it is not punitive and that public services are restored as well.[69]

Throughout Syria since the very beginning of the democratic uprising, communities have attempted with more or less success to establish civilian governance and prevent anarchy. The Local Coordination Committees (LCC) realized the importance of remaining committed to the original goals of the revolution—freedom, justice and equality for Syrians of all backgrounds. A network of 70 coordination groups (*tansiqiyat*) operated by media and street activists connected to the grassroots revolt inside Syria, played a key role in organizing anti-regime demonstrations, and disseminating information about the revolution.[70]

Activists in coordination committees across the country deplored the actions of warlords who are benefiting from the current conflict at the expense of the Syrian people. "They are no different from the corrupt regime," and have "sold the revolution for their personal gain," the grassroots organization said in a recent statement.[71] However, the dwindling secular opposition in Syria, whose activists have, in many cases, lost hope and fled the country, has given way to the uncertain control of the rebels in areas where civil services have broken down completely.

Unlike ISIS, the Al Nusrah Front seems to have a strong appreciation of the need to win hearts and minds to justify their presence in towns and villages under their control. They claim to control parts of at least a dozen Syrian towns, including sections of the ancient city of Aleppo in the northwest. The group's social wing, Qism al-Ighatha (Relief Department), provides food and warm clothing to civilians where possible, as well as seizing wheat by force to distribute among the hungry in Aleppo. The group has also released videos on jihadist websites claiming that it is providing services to the people of several towns in the governorate of Idlib, which borders the Aleppo Governorate to the west. Al Nusrah claims that it is a quasi-government and service provider in the towns of Binnish, Taum, and Saraqib.[72]

Aaron Zelin at the Washington Institute for Near East Policy says that Al Nusrah's ability to provide security and basic needs such as bread and fuel to Syrian civilians, as well as to reopen shops and restart bus services, has won gratitude from people who would not usually adhere to its strict ideology.

> This seems to demonstrate that we are witnessing the building of JN security structures across the country, showing that the group are adapting to the changing conflict, and making preparations for a post-Assad future by taking steps towards separate security service and army structures. JN's sharia courts are also open to Syrian civilians, and non-members have come to ask the court's advice on personal matters. The Free Syrian Army (FSA) recently adopted a similar legal

structure, with an FSA member explaining the benefits of establishing a court as a way of maintaining law and order.[73]

The Front's behavior in Deraa, demonstrated by its insistence on collaboration and lack of conflict with other rebel groups, indicates that the group is responsive to local conditions and able to "play by the rules" in a given battle space.[74] This gains it some credibility with the exiled opposition leadership who disagree with the U.S. designation of the Al Nusrah Front as a terrorist organization.[75]

By contrast, the other al-Qaeda affiliate, ISIS, is despised by many Syrians, as its goal seems to be not to defeat Assad but to consolidate its own power in rebel-held areas. This has led to its recent denunciation by rebel groups and the demand that it disband and leave the country. Syria represented al-Qaeda's best chance of proving its continuing relevance by establishing a new base in the Middle East. ISIS has ruined this opportunity by its hesitancy in taking on Assad's forces and by moving in to already liberated areas and proving to be more barbaric than the Assad regime.[76]

In this respect, at least within basically Arab and Sunni communities, it may appear that al-Qaeda has learned its lessons from Iraq. It has taken from the long-established Muslim Brotherhood and groups like Hamas and Hizbollah an appreciation of the importance of acting as a source of security and food, as well as being a combat force. The problem, of course, is that on religious grounds, it can make no appeal to Shia, Christian, or secular communities and seems to have lost any chance of alliance with the Kurdish communities of northern Syria.

SYRIA TODAY

The extent that al-Qaeda can manage this balance between gaining at least the tolerance of the wider population, and its own core ideology is perhaps the key to understanding the true strength of its recent resurgence. In early-2013, the Canadian Security Intelligence Service (CSIS) commissioned a workshop of experts to assess the future of al-Qaeda. CSIS found: "How AQ [al-Qaeda] adapts to the challenges and opportunities that will shape its next decade is a source of spirited debate amongst government officials, academic experts, think-tank analysts and private consultants."[77]

The "spirited debate" will persist as the conflict in Syria continues to reveal the intransigence and the growing isolation of the now discredited and ostracized al-Qaeda faction, ISIS. ISIS retains control of various areas in Syria and, according to analyst Aron Lund, will probably resist pressure to abandon them.[78] How the other al-Qaeda faction, the Al Nusrah Front, reacts to this development will be an indication of al-Qaeda's remaining strength and influence in Syria. The Al Nusrah Front is showing more flexibility and cooperation with the other salafi-jihadi alliances as, after all, they share the same ideology. But their allegiance to al-Zawahiri sets them apart from the other alliances' command structures. Until they embrace the authority of the Sharia tribunals being established, they run the risk of being isolated like ISIS.[79] Most Syrians see this as a struggle against the Assad regime, not as part of a wider al-Qaeda goal to re-establish territorial control of a significant portion of the Muslim world.

In the meantime, the resurgence of AQI is causing great disquiet. A December 2013 report by Dr.

Michael Knights of the Washington Institute for Near East Policy stresses the necessity of defeating the al-Qaeda narrative in Iraq and "splitting the reconcilable Sunnis from irreconcilable militants."[80]

This is happening in Syria with the now overt battle of the jihadist militias against the "irreconcilable militants" of the rebel al-Qaeda affiliate, ISIS. A statement from the Front of Syrian Revolutionaries shows its antagonism towards ISIS, which is referred to as Daash, the acronym in Arabic for ISIS.[81] Jaysh al-Mujahideen is a coalition of seven Islamist factions that announced its formation on January 2, 2014. Their statement also makes it clear that they consider ISIS the enemy:

> We, the army of Mujahideen announce that in defense of ourselves, our honor, our money and our land, we declare war on ISIS so long as it refuses to obey God's law until which time it dissolves and its members join other military groups or they leave their weapons and quit Syria.[82]

A January 4, 2014, report out of Beirut by Agence Presse added that the Alliance reproached ISIS for:

> spreading strife and insecurity . . . in liberated [rebel] areas, spilling the blood of fighters and wrongly accusing them of heresy, and expelling them and their families from areas they have paid heavily to free from Assad's forces.

The report went on to say that "At least 36 members and supporters of ISIS have been killed since Friday in Idlib, and more than 100 have been captured by rebels" in Idlib and Aleppo, the Syrian Observatory for Human Rights said.[83]

Hassan Aboud, political head of the Islamic Front, explained the tensions in a recent Al Jazeera interview.

We would like these [ISIS] brothers to join their brethren in the Syrian revolution. We see them as nothing but another group. They see themselves as a State. They need to drop this illusion that they have come to believe as an established fact. It causes them to treat allies as opponents. Nusra doesn't differ in ideology and authority from ISIS, but they have been able to work hand in glove with the other militias because they have followed the rule that no objective has a higher priority than pushing back the enemy. So we call on ISIS to follow Nusra's lead.[84]

The Islamic Front makes it quite clear that the common goal should be of establishing an Islamic state and deciding its leadership and governance comes after the defeat of Assad's forces. The Emir of ISIS, Abu Bakr al-Baghdadi, obviously has been premature and arbitrary in designating himself the Caliph[85] and demanding that others give him allegiance.

It now remains to be seen how the Al Nusrah Front fills the vacuum created by the loss of credibility and likely demise of ISIS. However, the problems of ISIS are not necessarily a blow to al-Qaeda, an affront to its leader al-Zawahiri, and a public relations disaster for its objective of establishing a global caliphate. Al Nusrah is formally aligned to al-Qaeda and presumably sees the principle gain from victory in Syria the establishment of a safe region that has been al-Qaeda's goal since it was evicted from Afghanistan. It is being more tactically astute than ISIS in short-term cooperation with the wider jihadist alliances in Syria but presumably retains very separate long-term goals.

The other groups may have some awareness of this, as the Islamic Alliance has since it was superseded by a new Islamic Front, as announced in November 2013.

Seven rebel groups came together in a new configuration that excludes the al-Qaeda affiliated Al Nusrah Front. It includes the Tawheed Brigade and the salafist Ahrar al Sham and thus potentially brings together tens of thousands of fighters. The leader of the new Alliance is Abu Eissa al-Sheikh, who described the new coalition on Al Jazeera as an "independent political, military and social formation . . . to topple the Assad regime . . . and to build an Islamic state."[86]

Since the announcement of the new Islamic Front, two new coalitions have been announced in January 2014, called Jaysh al-Mujahideen and the Front of Syrian Revolutionaries, the new configurations being formed as a backlash against ISIS. The Syrian Opposition Coalition has also spoken out against ISIS, calling it "a regime inspired organization, designed to undermine the revolution and pervert the meaning of Islam."[87]

> The Coalition stands in full solidarity with all Syrians rising up against al-Qaeda's extremism and calls upon the international community to recognize the importance of supporting revolutionary forces as partners in the fight against al-Qaeda's extremism and Assad's sponsorship and encouragement of extremist forces.[88]

Opposed by all other forces in Syria, ISIS seems to have backed itself into an ideological corner, leaving the Al Nusrah Front as the remaining al-Qaeda standard bearer.

CONCLUSION

The war in Syria has become a complex network of conflicts. The regime has brought in fighters from Hizbollah, threatening to spread the war to Lebanon. The anti-Assad opposition is split between secular groups such as the FSA, Islamists such as the Islamist Front, and the two competing al-Qaeda factions of ISIS and the Al Nusrah Front. Division between the FSA, the al-Qaeda elements, and the salafi-jihadists has created a tenuous situation, with rival Islamist factions intent on establishing their own territorial spheres of influence, thus enabling Assad's forces to regroup and fight back. The new alliance against ISIS should help to rally support from overseas and to raise morale.

However, it is not just a domestic dispute but has become a proxy war between Saudi Arabia and Iran, with involvement also of Qatar, Turkey, and Iraq.[89] Until all these nations stop funding and arming the opposing groups, the war will continue indefinitely since it is clear the Assad regime has the capacity to resist but lacks the ability to re-establish complete control. While the war continues, Syria is an incubator of salafi-jihadist extremism that is threatening the internal stability of Muslim countries with Sunni and Shia populations. According to Aron Lund, editor of the *Syria in Crisis* website run by the Carnegie Endowment, "the two conflicts in Iraq and Syria are melting into one. The more conflicts you pull into the Syria war the harder it will be to stop it."[90] But peace should be an imperative, not an option.

As the winter advances and the rebel forces gains are countered by Assad forces retaking positions to cut rebel supply lines, the war seems to have reached a stalemate. The resilience of the Assad regime is dispiriting the activists who created the revolution nearly 3 years ago. Disillusioned by the lack of support from the West, the corruption of rebel commanders, the disarray and division on their side, and the rising power of the Islamist rebels, many are exhausted by the conflict, which has no end in sight.

The battle now is one of survival rather than a fight for democracy and civil rights. As many young motivated people are leaving the country, it becomes even harder for those who remain. Stories of betrayal and disappointment are common, and the only hope for Syria today is for negotiations to bring about a ceasefire, while the weakened Assad regime still maintains the remnants of statehood and thus represents a body with which to negotiate. The revolution has failed, but equally so, the Assad regime has failed to win mass support.[91] The protracted civil war has created a rapidly failing state, a tragic refugee problem, and it is estimated that by the end of 2014, more than half the population of Syria will be living as refugees, a situation that can only be resolved by the powers who are enabling it to continue.[92]

The United States has provided substantial amounts of nonlethal as well as military aid, especially to the FSA. However, this was suspended when the FSA lost control of key stocks to the Islamist groups and subsequently nonlethal aid was restarted. However, the United States has found another avenue to send weapons by sending 15,000 anti-tank missiles to Saudi Arabia, at a cost of over $1 billion. The expectation is that Saudi will retain these to modernize its forces and will send its older stockpiles to the Syrian rebels.[93] The Islamic coalitions will welcome the arms to continue the war of attrition against Assad's artillery and air power, with the recent barrel bomb attacks in Aleppo suggesting that Assad is running out of sophisticated weaponry. However, the insurgents are still facing a bleak winter, with erratic supplies and with the added complication of ISIS no longer as an ally and, in some cases, as the enemy. However, this suggests that enough arms will reach Syria to allow the various factions to continue to fight, even if there is no longer a realistic hope that the war will end by military victory.

Al-Qaeda's future is tied up with these dynamics. The attempt by ISIS to create an Islamic state of Greater Syria has been discredited, and its fighters will probably eventually retreat across the border to Iraq to join the al-Qaeda led insurgency there. The question remains of how long the al-Qaeda resurgence will last and whether it has the staying power to remain in areas where it now has armed control. Equally, although the Al Nusrah Front is formally aligned to al-Qaeda's central leadership, at the moment it is operating in relatively close cooperation with the salafist Islamic Front and is seeking to balance its military goals with building a social system in areas it controls.

If al-Qaeda is to be denied a foothold, it will be essential for the new Islamic Front to hold together and continue to occupy the moral high ground, so that it may increasingly be seen as separate and distinct from al-Qaeda, represented now only by the Al Nusrah Front. The banishing of ISIS has presumably had the effect of weakening the al-Qaeda presence and prestige in Syria and reinforces the ascendancy of coalitions, with or without the Al Nusrah Front. The statement announcing the Islamic Front described it as "an independent political, military, and social formation that seeks to completely topple the Assad regime in Syria and build an orthodox Islamic state."[94] Most of the participating groups have cooperated in battle in the past, and, while one spokesman denied that the alliance had been formed to challenge ISIS, it has been perceived as a show of force by mainline rebel factions against the al-Qaeda extremists.

Former U.S. Ambassador to Syria Robert Stephen Ford established contact with the new Islamic Front leaders in November, and the Obama administration has committed itself to "an expanded Syrian insurgency that includes the recently-formed Islamic Front."[95] This can be interpreted as a pragmatic decision to ensure that the Al Nusrah Front is marginalized from the wider Islamist opposition. However, this suggests that the U.S. administration simply does not know what to do, or who to support, and that every option looks like a bad one.

"The conflict has become an existential struggle for all concerned and not even the fall of Assad will bring an end to the violence."[96] Local militias are operating beyond any rules of engagement and have not yet come together to make the transition from guerilla fighters to a force capable of defeating Assad's army on the ground. Fighting continues with uncoordinated autonomous formations attaining tactical victories but unable to alter the situation strategically.

U.S. policy will have to change as nonintervention has made the situation worse.[97] It is a supreme irony that the United States, after spending so much time, treasure, and so many lives to defeat terrorism, may now have to ally itself with salafi-jihadis to topple Assad and end the carnage in Syria. As the Islamic Front has not been designated a terrorist organization like the Al Nusrah Front, the United States can create closer relationships with secular and moderate rebels in the Islamic Front, avoiding any hint of support for Assad and developing an understanding of what the grassroots Syrian population has been trying to achieve. In the process, it could continue to weaken al-Qaeda until it is a marginalized branch of a much bigger enterprise of concern — the growing salafi-jihadi movement. In the meantime:

> The longer the Syrians fight, the more sectarian the conflict becomes, the more savage the fighting, the more sectarian cleansing will occur, the greater the accumulation of reasons for revenge, the less likely there is to be a political situation.[98]

This leaves open the future of al-Qaeda and its desire to establish an Islamic state in Iraq and Syria. ISIS has failed to impose its will in Syria but remains the dominant power in northern Iraq. In turn, the Al Nusrah Front is the dominant al-Qaeda faction in Syria but has no influence in Iraq. The traditional al-Qaeda approach, typified by ISIS, has little chance of gaining popular support beyond those fully committed. Its brutality and sectarianism preclude even tactical alliances, and its ideological straightjacket means its version of Sharia law loses it any support in regions it controls. In this respect, the Al Nusrah Front may be a more formidable foe. It seems to have learned the importance of building a social support network and close cooperation with those who share much of its ideology. Equally, it seems to have accepted the Islamic Front's logic: essentially win the war first, and then work out the nature of the state. On the other hand, ISIS stressed its differences with any other ideological or religious current even while the war with Assad's regime was ongoing.

The U.S. administration's decision to not proscribe the Islamic Front, as well as the Islamic Front's need to retain its Gulf backers, may mean the current loose alliance with Al Nusrah is doomed. Faced with the risk to its funding and arms supplies if it continues to operate in tandem, the Islamic Front may well turn on its al-Qaeda ally. Equally, the Islamic Front is essentially fighting a domestic struggle in Syria, while Al Nusrah, given its allegiance to the core al-Qaeda leadership, presumably sees Syria as simply a means to an end — the re-establishment of a safe zone the organization has lacked since it was evicted from Afghanistan.

Even if the alliance is maintained, Al Nusrah will struggle to balance its military and social roles. Jacob Shapiro, in his book *The Terrorists Dilemma*, discusses the problem that terrorist organizations face to maintain organizational discipline and management, "given the secretive nature and the challenges and constraints of communication without detection."[99] Also when commanders in the field become too independent, it is difficult for the leadership to control them except by cutting off funds, which further alienates the commanders who then tend to resort to kidnapping, smuggling, or the drug trade to finance their operations. This brings the name of salafi-jihadism and al-Qaeda further into disrepute among moderate peace-loving Muslims.

Shapiro refers to the mundane side of terrorism, such as the bookkeeping, the disciplinary procedures, and recruiting processes that make them similar to ordinary organizations, yet they are unique in that they operate at a tremendous disadvantage.

> The difficult task is achieving the controlled use of violence as a means of achieving a specified political end. Using too much violence, or hitting the wrong targets, can be just as damaging to the cause as employing too little.[100]

The problems of becoming detached from the field because of having to maintain security have led to a lack of confidence in leadership, resulting in internal conflicts and schisms, clearly evident in Syria right now. Problems of trust and control have been issues plaguing al-Qaeda for many years, according to captured documents in the U.S. Department of Defense's Harmony Database. Based on these documents, Shapiro says:

> At the end of the day, these examples will highlight that terrorists are, for the most part, not nearly as successful or committed as the most successful of their kind might make one think. As a result, their organizations are nothing close to the threat that many in the policy community once claimed them to be.[101]

However, even if Al Nusrah is isolated and collapses under the tensions of its contradictions, this assumes that the war continues. One fear now is of fighters from Syria returning to their original countries. All those countries whose nationals are at present fighting in Syria under various insurgents' banners have a vested interest in not wanting them to return home with their dangerous expertise and experience. On January 1, 2014, The Meir Amit Intelligence and Terrorism Information Center published a definitive report on the numbers of foreign jihadis at present in Syria and their nationalities, and stressed the potential danger to the Western world.[102]

According to Peter Bergen, CNN's national security analyst, the widening reach of al-Qaeda in the Middle East does not necessarily translate into an immediate threat for the United States as "only a handful of Americans have fought in the Syrian conflict alongside al-Qaeda's affiliates." However, his January 8, 2014, report says that hundreds of European citizens have been fighting in Syria, and there is a valid concern that the returning veterans of the Syrian conflict might launch terrorist attacks in Europe.[103] The United States and its allies should therefore make a careful effort to track the foreign fighters who have joined jihadist groups fighting in Syria.

Given the consequences of the war continuing, urgent consideration must be given to negotiating a ceasefire and supporting peace talks. However, the rather tenuous statements from the U.S. administration reveal nothing but cautious optimism about the current peace talks in Geneva, Switzerland. Apart from the Syrian National Council, most factions have refused to attend the self-declared "government in exile" opposing the regime of President Bashar al-Assad. Secretary of State John Kerry called recent negotiations "a big step forward and a significant one,"[104] but did not immediately address how the conflicting demands would be resolved. At the same time, the United States continues to supply weapons indirectly to the conflict , as do the Sunni Gulf states and Iran.

One key issue is what the Syrian conflict tells us about the trajectory and influence of al-Qaeda. It is clear the organization has the capacity to embed itself into any conflict, and its trained, motivated fighters give it influence beyond its small numbers. There are some signs that the Al Nusrah Front has tried to learn from the sectarianism that has limited its appeal in Iraq where a combination of indiscriminate attacks and a harsh interpretation of Sharia law means few give the group real support. On the other hand, there is ample evidence that the central al-Qaeda leadership is struggling to maintain control, and the loss of ISIS is a warning that local affiliates can become self-sufficient. That does not end the appeal of the ideology but does indicate that al-Qaeda is now struggling to maintain control over its various regional movements. In Syria, it is likely that the Islamist Front will turn on its allies, not the least as this may be the price paid to maintain access to U.S. and Gulf State funds and weapons.

However, even in this case, it is more likely that most Al Nusrah fighters and local commanders will be co-opted into the Islamic Front rather than driven from Syria. Al-Qaeda, as an organization, may well find that the Syrian civil war points to the limits of its influence. What the Syrian civil war will not do is to end the appeal of the wider salafist-jihadist ideology.

SOURCES

Al-Qaeda in the United States, Cambridge, UK: The Henry Jackson Society, 2013.

Council on Foreign Relations, Washington, DC.

Higgins, Eliot. Brown Moses blog, *brown-moses.blogspot.com/*.

Institute for the Study of War, Washington, DC. See *www.understandingwar.org/*.

The International Center for the Study of Radicalization and Political Violence, London, UK.

The International Crisis Group, Brussels, Belgium.

Jenkins, Brian Michael. *The Dynamics of Syria's Civil War*, Santa Monica, CA: Rand Corporation. Available from *www.rand.org/content/dam/rand/pubs/perspectives/PE100/PE115/RAND_PE115.pdf*.

Jihadica. Available from *www.jihadica.com/*.

Landis, Joshua, *Syriacomment.com*.

The Long War Journal. Available from *www.longwarjournal.org/*.

Lund, Aron. *Syria's Salafi Insurgents: The Rise of the Syrian Islamic Front*. Available from *www.ui.se/eng/upl/files/86861.pdf*.

The Meir Amit Intelligence and Terrorism Information Center, Gelilot, Israel.

The Middle East Media Research Institute, Washington, DC.

The Quilliam Foundation, London, UK.

"The Resurgence of al-Qaeda in Iraq," Joint Subcommittee Hearing, Subcommittee on Terrorism, Nonproliferation, and Trade, Washington, DC, December 12, 2013.

Shumukh al-Islam, al-Qaeda's semi-official online forum.

SITE Monitoring Service. See *news.siteintelgroup.com/*.

Syria in Crisis. Washington, DC: The Carnegie Endowment for International Peace. Available from *carnegieendowment.org/syriaincrisis/?fa=54233*.

Syria Untold. Available from *www.syriauntold.com/en/story/2013/10/04/5527.*

White, Jeffrey, Andrew J. Tabler, and Aaron Y. Zelin. *Syria's Military Opposition: How Effective, United, or Extremist?* POLICY FOCUS 128, Washington, DC: The Washington Institute, September 2013.

ENDNOTES

1. Donald Rumsfeld, 2103, quoted in *usatoday30.usatoday.com/news/washington/executive/rumsfeld-memo.htm*.

2. See *nation.time.com/2011/06/29/the-5-trillion-war-on-terror/# comments*.

3. See *www.aljazeera.com/indepth/interactive/2013/12/timeline-arab-spring-20131217114018534352.html*.

4. Mary Anne Weaver, in a profile of Osama bin Laden, *The New Yorker*, January 24, 2000.

5. Gaith Abdul-Ahad, "Syria is not a revolution anymore— this is civil war," *The Guardian*, November 18, 2013.

6. Thomas Joscelyn "Global al Qaeda: Affiliates, Objectives, and Future Challenges," *The Long War Journal*, July 18, 2013.

7. See *cnsnews.com/news/article/obama-touts-al-qaeda-s-demise-32-times-benghazi-attack-0*.

8. Barry Rubin, "Why the CIA is wrong, Rethinking Al Qaeda," *RubinReports*, February 22, 2013.

9. Peter Bergen, "Should we still fear Al Qaeda?" CNN, February 6, 2013.

10. See *www.youtube.com/watch?v=jlubL-dIJ0s*.

11. Jacob Shapiro, *The Terrorists Dilemma*, Princeton, NJ: Princeton University Press, 2013, p. 15.

12. See *www.youtube.com/watch?v=jlubL-dIJ0s*.

13. Bruce Reidel, "Kenya Terror Strike Was Part of Al-Qaeda's Latest Global Jihad," *New Age Islam*, October 2, 2013.

14. Mary Anne Weaver, in a profile of Osama bin Laden, *The New Yorker*, January 24, 2000.

15. The Associated Press, "Al Qaeda records even the most minute expenses including 60 cents for cake," *Daily News*, March 17, 2014. Also see *www.nydailynews.com/news/world/al-qaeda-documents-show-real-company-infrastructure-article-1.1560804#ixzz2wF-7DJ4Pk*.

16. Joscelyn.

17. William McCants, as quoted in *Ibid*.

18. Joscelyn.

19. David Kirkpatrick, "A Deadly Mix in Benghazi," *The New York Times*, December 28, 2013.

20. Guy Taylor, "Intel community: NY Times wrong, al Qaeda links in Benghazi are clear," *The Washington Times*, December 30, 2013.

21. There is a substantial archive of translated material at the Combating Terrorism Center at West Point, NY. One relevant report is available from *www.ctc.usma.edu/posts/self-inflicted-wounds*.

22. Abdel Moneim Al Moshawah, "Zawahiri speech, though confused, shows U.S. is still main al-Qaeda target," Dubai, United Arab Emirates: Al Arabiya Institute, October 8, 2013.

23. See *www.ctc.usma.edu/posts/zawahiris-letter-to-zarqawi-english-translation-2*.

24. "The Doctor's advice: Zawahiri issues 'jihad guidelines'," *The Dawn*, September 19, 2013.

25. William McCants, "How Zawahiri Lost al Qaeda: Global Jihad Turns on Itself," *Foreign Affairs*, November 19, 2013.

26. Jacob Shapiro, p. 18.

27. See *www.joshualandis.com/blog/#_ftn12*.

28. Dr. Joshua M. Landis, Director of the Center of Middle Eastern Studies, University of Oklahoma, Norman, OK, telephone interview, January 3, 2014.

29. Daniel Nisman, "A New Islamist Alliance Among Syria's Rebels. The creation of the Islamic Alliance has the potential to make anti-Assad moderates extinct," *The Wall Street Journal*, September 26, 2013.

30. Agence-France, "New rebel alliance wants Syria as 'Islamic state'," *Hurriyet*, March 18, 2014.

31. Joshua Landis, *Syriacomment.com*, October 1, 2013.

32. See *carnegieendowment.org/syriaincrisis/?fa=54233*.

33. Hassan Hassan, "The Army of Islam is Winning in Syria," *Foreign Policy*, October 2, 2013.

34. Interview by the author with Michael Weiss, January 15, 2014.

35. Cole Bunzel, "Al-Qaeda Advises the Syrian Revolution: Shumukh al-Islam's 'Comprehensive Strategy' for Syria," *Jihadica*, February, 25, 2013.

36. The Meir Amit Intelligence and Terrorism Information Center, September 23, 2013.

37. Elizabeth O'Baqy, "Jihad in Syria," Security Report No. 6, September 2012, p. 23.

38. Michael Knights, "The Resurgence of Al Qaeda in Iraq," Testimony to the House Committee on Foreign Affairs, Washington, DC: U.S. House of Representatives, December 12, 2013.

39. Isabel Nassief, "The Campaign for Homs and Aleppo," Washington, DC: Institute for Study of War, January 28, 2014.

40. "Iraq city seizures illustrate Qaeda group's resurgence," *Space War*, January 5, 2014, available from *www.spacewar.com/reports/Iraq_city_seizures_illustrate_Qaeda_groups_resurgence_999.html*.

41. Jessica D. Lewis, "Al Qaeda in Iraq Resurgent," Washington, DC: Institute for Study of War, September 2013.

42. While most foreign attention has been on the Shia Hizbollah, there has been a long-standing problem with al-Qaeda related groups, especially in the northern port city of Tripoli. The potential for this division to form the basis of outright conflict in Lebanon is substantial.

43. "Fighting in Iraq's Anbar kills at least 32," *Al Arabiya News*, January 3, 2014.

44. See *foreignaffairs.house.gov/hearing/joint-subcommittee-hearing-resurgence-al-qaeda-iraq.*

45. *Ibid.*

46. See *en.alalam.ir/news/1532838#sthash.PxCzHG1F.dpuf.*

47. Joas Wagemakers, "Al Qaida advises the Arab Spring: The Case for al-Baghdadi," *Jihidica*, September 21, 2013.

48. Suhaib Anjarini, "The evolution of al-Qaeda; From Iraq to Syria," *Alalam*, November 9, 2013.

49. Landis, *Syriacomment.com.*

50. "Syrian Kurds Regain Control of Strategic Regions in Hasaka Province," Fars News Agency, November 27, 2013.

51. Cole Bunzel, "The Islamic State of Disobedience: al-Baghdadi Triumphant," *Jihadica*, October 5, 2013.

52. See *rt.com/news/al-qaeda-syria-disbanded-480/.*

53. BBC, "Al-Qaeda disavows ISIS militants in Syria," BBC, February 3, 2014.

54. Bunzel.

55. William McCants, "How Zawahiri Lost Al Qaeda," Washington, DC: Brookings Foreign Affairs, November 19, 2013, p. 30, available from *www.brookings.edu/research/opinions/2013/11/19-how-zawahri-lost-al-qaeda-mccantsw.*

56. See *www.nybooks.com/blogs/nyrblog/2013/dec/27/how-al-qaeda-changed-syrian-war/*.

57. See *www.joshualandis.com/blog/al-qaedas-governance-strategy-raqqa-chris-looney/*.

58. Norman Benotman and Roisin Blake, *Jabat al-Nusra*, London, UK: Quilliam Foundation, September 25, 2012.

59. David Trifunov, "Abu Mohammad al-Golani, leader of Jabhat al-Nusra, killed in Syria, state TV claims," Global Post, October 25, 2013.

60. Benotman and Blake.

61. *Ibid.*

62. *Ibid.*, p. 85.

63. See *www.nybooks.com/blogs/nyrblog/2013/dec/27/how-al-qaeda-changed-syrian-war/?insrc=wbll*.

64. The Meir Amit Intelligence and Terrorism Information Center, Gelilot, Israel.

65. Marian Karouny, "Syria's Nusra rebels say support Qaeda's Zawahri," *Reuters*, April 10, 2013.

66. Benotman and Blake.

67. *Ibid.*

68. Phil Greaves, "Syria: 'The Army of Islam'; Saudi Arabia's Greatest Export," Global Research, October 3, 2013.

69. Interview by the author with Aron Lund, January 6, 2013.

70. See *carnegieendowment.org/syriaincrisis/?fa=Coalitions&lang=en*.

71. See *www.lccsyria.org/category/news*.

72. See *www.cnn.com/2014/01/07/opinion/bergen-al-qaeda-terror-ity-gains/index.html*.

73. Benotman and Blake.

74. Nassief.

75. See *www.nybooks.com/blogs/nyrblog/2013/dec/27/how-al-qaeda-changed-syrian-war/?insrc=wbll*.

76. Interview by the author with Michael Weiss, January 15, 2014.

77. Joscelyn.

78. Interview by the author with Aron Lund, January 6, 2013.

79. *Ibid.*

80. See *foreignaffairs.house.gov/hearing/joint-subcommittee-hearing-resurgence-al-qaeda-iraq*.

81. Joshua Landis, "The Battle between ISIS and Syria's Rebel Militias," *Syria Comment*, January 4, 2014.

82. *Ibid.*

83. *Al Arabiya News*, January 4, 2014.

84. Landis, "The Battle between ISIS and Syria's Rebel Militias."

85. R. Green, "The Rift in the Global Jihad Movement," *The Counter Jihad Report*, February 21, 2014. Note that al-Baghdadi is described as having "designated himself as a global leader of the jihad fighters in particular and of Muslims in general, and as a herald of the Caliphate."

86. Loveday Morris, "Seven Syrian Islamist Groups form new Islamic Front," *The Washington Post*, November 22, 2013.

87. Landis, "The Battle between ISIS and Syria's Rebel Militias."

88. See *english.alarabiya.net/en/News/middle-east/2014/01/04/New-Syria-rebel-alliance-declares-war-on-al-Qaeda.html.*

89. Jeremy Shapiro and Samual Sharap, *Theguardian.com*, November 26, 2013.

90. Interview by the author with Aron Lund, January 6, 2013.

91. Joseph Halliday, "The Assad Regime: From Counterinsurgency to Civil War," *Middle East Journal*, March 2013.

92. Brian Michael Jenkins, *The Dynamics of Syria's Civil War*, Santa Monica, CA: Rand Perspective, November 2013.

93. Tony Cartalucci, *Syria's War: The Next Phase*, available from *www.informationclearinghouse.info/article37121.htm.*

94. Abu Eissa al-Sheikh, leader of the new entity, as he announced the group's creation on Al Jazeera.

95. Michel Chossudovsky, "Washington's New Islamic Front: Expanded U.S. Support to Al Qaeda Rebels in Syria," *Global Research*, January 28, 2014.

96. Jenkins.

97. Interview by the author with Michael Weiss, January 15, 2014.

98. *Ibid.*

99. Jacob Shapiro.

100. *Ibid.*

101. *Ibid.*, p. 10.

102. See *www.terrorism-info.org.il/en/article/20607.*

103. See *www.cnn.com/2014/01/07/opinion/bergen-al-qaeda-terrority-gains/index.html.*

104. See *live.aljazeera.com/Event/Syria_Live_Blog?Page=14.*

APPENDIX

AL-QAEDA IN OTHER PARTS OF THE WORLD

A detailed report by Thomas Joscelyn was presented to the U.S. Senate Foreign Relations Committee on November 21, 2013, regarding al-Qaeda's network in Africa and the threat it poses to the United States.

AL-QAEDA IN THE MAGREB (AQIM)

AQIM, in his opinion, is still a very viable organization and, like Islamic State in Iraq and Syria (ISIS) in Syria, is restless under al-Zawahiri's control. The leader of one of the AQIM brigades, Mokhtar Belmokhtar, refused to work with other AQIM leaders in North Africa and pledged allegiance directly to al-Zawahiri. In August 2012, Belmokhtar announced that his group, the al-Mulathameen Brigade, had merged with the Movement for Unity and Jihad in West Africa (MUJAO).

> The AQIM network includes groups that are frequently identified as 'local' jihadist organizations. It is widely believed that groups such as Ansar al-Dine and the Ansar al Sharia chapters are not really a part of the al Qaeda network in North and West Africa.[1]

However, despite disagreements between the leaders of these various al-Qaeda-linked groups, according to Joscelyn, they are all openly loyal to al-Qaeda's senior leadership, and they have all continued to work closely together in Mali and elsewhere. In addition, Boko Haram, which was also recently designated a terrorist organization, has joined this coalition and is "linked" to AQIM.[2]

Ansar al Sharia in Egypt, Libya, and Tunisia

Two prominent chapters of Ansar al Sharia (Partisans of Islamic Law) have risen in North Africa, one in Libya and the other in neighboring Tunisia. Some have argued that, while these Ansar al Sharia chapters cooperate with al-Qaeda, they have fundamentally different goals. Ansar al Sharia is said to be focused on purely "local" matters, while al-Qaeda is only interested in the global jihad. But this is simply not true. Al-Qaeda's most senior leaders, including Ayman al-Zawahiri, have repeatedly said that one of his organization's chief priorities is to implement Sharia law as the foundation for an Islamic state. This is precisely Ansar al Sharia's goal. In addition, there are credible reports that the Ansar al Sharia chapters in both Libya and Tunisia have provided recruits for al-Qaeda's affiliates and other jihadist organizations in Syria, the new epicenter for the global jihad.

> The weight of the evidence makes it far more likely than not that the Ansar al Sharia chapters in Egypt, Libya and Tunisia are part of al Qaeda's network in North Africa. This has important policy ramifications because both groups have been involved in violence, with Ansar al Sharia Libya taking part in the Benghazi terrorist attack and Ansar al Sharia Tunisia sacking the U.S. Embassy in Tunis 3 days later. The Tunisian government has also blamed Ansar al Sharia for a failed suicide attack, the first inside Tunisia in years. While both chapters have been involved in violence, they have also been working hard to earn new recruits for their organizations and al Qaeda's ideology. The Arab uprisings created a unique opportunity for them to proselytize.[3]

This assessment by Joscelyn has been confirmed by the Pentagon's own terrorism research agency, which concluded in August 2012 that "al-Qaeda senior leadership" based in Pakistan was "likely seeking to build a clandestine network in Libya as it pursues its strategy of reinforcing its presence in North Africa." The report predicted that AQIM was "likely to join hands with the al Qaeda clandestine network."[4]

A report by the Council on Foreign Relations, updated on January 8, 2014, notes that "though AQIM and its offshoots pose the primary transnational terror threat in North and West Africa, they are unlikely to strike US or Western interests beyond the region."[5] Spain and France are its foremost "far enemies" because of colonial history. The report also says that the merger with al-Qaeda may have discredited AQIM because of its association with the brutal tactics of al-Qaeda. in Iraq.

Egypt

Ansar al Sharia in Egypt has existed for some time, run mainly by former members of the Egyptian Islamic Jihad (EIJ), a terrorist organization headed by Ayman al-Zawahiri that merged with al-Qaeda. In July 2013, the formation of a new front was announced in the wake of Egyptian President Mohamed Morsi's ouster, according to the Search for International Terrorist Entities (SITE) Intelligence Group. The front is also called, "Ansar al Sharia in Egypt" and may be "a new front with the same name. Or, perhaps it is a new brand for an effort that was already in the works."[6]

Somalia

The al-Shabaab organization in Somalia merged with al-Qaeda in early-2012. Bin Laden had cautioned against this before his death, noting that al-Shabaab's harsh implementation of Sharia law was alienating the Somali population. After Bin Laden's death, however, al-Zawahiri went ahead and accepted a pledge of loyalty from al-Shabaab leader, Ahmed Abdi Godane.

Al-Shabaab today is fractured into multiple rival factions, some based along clan lines and others ideological. An Agence France-Presse (AFP) report in June 2013 stated that al-Shabaab extremists had killed two of its own co-founders. In spite of the perception that al-Shabaab has been severely weakened inside Somalia, where it has lost territory over the past 2 years, Godane has strengthened his control over the group with his ruthless treatment of rivals and his new hardline, international agenda. Al-Shabaab has said it carried out the deadly assault on a shopping center in Nairobi on September 21, 2013, in which at least 68 people were killed.

Brookings Institute analyst Daniel Byman has detailed the extent to which al-Qaeda, through offshoots like al-Shabaab, remains alive in Africa and, in his opinion, has even prospered. In a paper last year titled *Breaking the Bonds Between Al-Qa'ida and Its Affiliate Organizations*, he stated:

> . . . Shebaab pledged support for Zawahiri after bin Laden's death and then in 2012 more formally joining al-Qa'ida by declaring Shebaab members 'will march with you as loyal soldiers'. Some fighters who had trained in al-Qa'ida camps in Afghanistan moved to Somalia to train members of the Shebaab, and the two groups currently cooperate closely on everything from

indoctrination and basic infantry skills to advanced training in explosives and assassination.[7]

Yemen

On January 14, 2010, Yemen declared open war on al-Qaeda in the Arabian Peninsula (AQAP). Yemen is currently contending with a Shia insurgency in the north and militant separatists in the south, with ensuing waves of violence. In May 2013, Yemen's main oil pipeline was blown up by militants claiming to be Ansar al Sharia, or a re-branding of AQAP. The U.S. drone strikes in Yemen have caused great controversy, as the successful targeting and killing of militant leaders has also killed an estimated 100-200 civilians, plus 36 children. The outrage against the United States is mirrored by outrage against al-Qaeda's offshoot, Ansar al Sharia, which claimed responsibility for killing an estimated 52 people in an attack on a military hospital in Sanaa. The United States has improved its drone technology recently, and hopefully the rate of civilian casualties will drop in Yemen as it has in Pakistan where the Central Intelligence Agency and the Joint Special Operations Command (JSOC) also carry out controversial and lethal drone strikes.

United States

The presence of al-Qaeda in the U.S. homeland has been thoroughly documented by the Henry Jackson Society in its report, *Al-Qaeda in the United States*, published in 2013 and acknowledged by General Michael Hayden as "a remarkable work." It details how the terrorist threat within the United States has developed, by profiling all al-Qaeda or al-Qaeda inspired terrorists who were convicted in U.S. courts (federal and military) or who participated in suicide attacks against the U.S. homeland between 1997 and 2011.

> Al-Qaeda in the United States profiles 171 individuals who were convicted for al-Qaeda related offenses or committed suicide attacks between 1997 and 2011. It provides statistical analysis on their background (such as age, nationality, occupation, education and whether they were a religious convert); data relating to types of offenses, type of charge and their subsequent sentence; outlines individual connections to other known terrorists or designated terrorist organizations; and studies whether these individuals had received terrorist training or had combat experience.[8]

While the total of 171 individuals convicted may appear like a "resurgence" in al-Qaeda activity , it also represents a reassuring resurgence in successful anti-terrorism detection in the United States.

It is conceivable that al-Qaeda activity in Syria and Iraq is emboldening al-Qaeda affiliates and sympathizers in Africa, Yemen, and across the Muslim world wherever they exist as the increased use of global media channels enables more communication and publicity. At the same time, increased pushback from anti-terrorism forces and increased negative publicity about their reckless brutality and civilian deaths, is also bringing al-Qaeda into disrepute. The focus in 2014, however, will be on Syria, where al-Qaeda has been hurt, and its progress has been checked for now. But it is far from destroyed.

THE NON AL-QAEDA INSURGENTS: SYRIA'S SALAFI-JIHADIS

Aron Lund documents in detail the rise of the Syrian Islamic Front (SIF) in his March 2013 report for the Swedish Institute of International Affairs. Also in his four-part series for the Carnegie Endowment for International Peace, he examines in detail the politics of the Islamic Front and its emerging strength as the most powerful coalition in Syria.

On December 21, 2012, the SIF announced its creation through a video, bringing together 11 factions, the most influential being the Ahrar al-Sham network. It shares salafi-jihadi ideology but it is clearly focused on Syria:

> ... it also tries to highlight a streak of pragmatism and moderation, intended to reassure both Syrians and foreign policymakers. In this way, it sets itself apart as an Islamist 'third way', different from both the most radical fringe of the uprising, and from its Western-backed Islamist mainstream.[9]

Hassan Abboud, the general head of Ahrar al-Sham, spearheaded the joint position of the new Islamic Alliance announced in November 2013, rejecting the Syrian National Council (SNC) and U.S. backed exile groups, as well as the two al-Qaeda affiliates. However, Abboud pulled out of the council shortly after the merger, criticizing "the hegemony of certain factions and the exclusion of [other] effective ones," referring to the exclusion of al-Qaeda's Al Nusrah Front. His statements since are seen to be an attempt to include the Al Nusrah Front and moderate it, rather than alienate it like ISIS.[10]

The success of any alliance or coalition attempting to be the "third way" between the Free Syrian Army (FSA) and more extremist militias like the Al Nusrah Front will depend on its ability to acquire a sufficient level of funding to sustain its ambitious bid for salafi leadership. Otherwise, it is likely to fragment with time, like so many Syrian rebel alliances before it.[11]

The Islamic Front brought together ideologically disparate groups: Ahrar al-Shaam (jihadi-salafi inclination), Suqur al-Shaam and Liwa' al-Tawhid (Muslim Brotherhood), Jaish al-Islam (salafi and former Muslim Brotherhood members with Saudi connections), and Liwa' al-Haqq,[12] to name a few.

Liwa al-Islam, the Army of Islam, is a coalition of about 50 insurgent groups operating around Damascus, which merged into Jaysh al–Islam, (Army of Islam). General Commander of Jaysh al-Islam, Zahran Alloush, is the son of a Saudi-based religious scholar, and his Army of Islam flies the black flag and not the Syrian flag. He speaks of resurrecting the Omayyad Empire and has little faith in democracy, seeking to establish an Islamic state ruled by a committee of Islamic scholars. He is suspicious of the FSA because of its links with Western countries. Saudi Arabia seems to be central to the new coalition. Liwa al-Islam was backed by Riyadh and is the central player in the Army of Islam.

According to Hassan Hassan in a *Foreign Policy* article:

> Although Liwa al-Islam had been part of the Saudi-backed FSA, the spokesman of the new grouping told an Arabic television channel that the Army of Islam is not part of the FSA. This is likely because the FSA has lost the trust of many rebel groups, and adopting a religious language will be more effective

in countering the appeal of radical groups—which is what happened after the announcement of the merger, as various Islamists and moderate groups welcomed the move.[13]

Contrary to the popular narrative emerging in Western and Gulf media that this new force will represent a "moderate Islamist" coalition capable of taking on al-Qaeda, the majority of Syrians will be repelled by the sectarian language and ideologies of Zohran Alloush, his group's overt affiliations, their pandering to al-Qaeda ideologues, and his "Army of Islam."[14]

Another group in Syria is the Abdullah Azzam Brigades, which is not recognized as a formal al-Qaeda affiliate, but it is openly loyal to al-Qaeda, and its leaders have long operated as part of the al-Qaeda network.[15] Majid bin Muhammad al-Majid, the Azzam Brigades' leader, in August 2013 called for Sunnis in Lebanon and Syria to unite against Hizbollah, which he calls the "party of Iran." The Azzam Brigades took responsibility for firing rockets at Israel and recently for the attack on the Iranian Embassy in Beirut, Lebanon, on November 19, 2013. Another example of the volatility of the situation is that it was announced on December 31, 2013, that Lebanese Armed Forces had recently captured Majid bin Muhammad al-Majid. A new leader will doubtless be announced for the Abdullah Azzam Brigades.

Some other leaders with broader appeal in the Arab and Islamist mainstream, in contrast with the al-Qaeda leaders, are:[16]

- Ahmad ʿAisa al-Shaykh, or Abu Aissa, commander of Suqour al-Sham Brigade, Falcons of Syria Brigade, based in Idlib.

- Abdul Qader Al-Saleh was the high Commander of Liwa al-Tawhid (Unity Brigade) based in Aleppo and is a large, umbrella movement formed out of regional militias numbering about 15,000 men. Killed in action in November 2013, Abdul Qader most likely will be succeeded by Abdelaziz Salame, who was wounded in the same attack. In a dispatch for *Syria Comment* on November 17, 2013, Aron Lund reported that:

> Leadership succession might not be an easy thing for such a group. It could suffer internal divisions and even violent strife, at the loss of a central and unifying leader. At a time when the Syrian regime is advancing on Aleppo, Saleh's death therefore is very bad news for the opposition. Even if the front holds, Tawhid could be drained of cohesion, and end up losing subunits and fighters to other groups.[17]

- Bashar Al-Zoubi, the Commander of Liwa al-Yarmouk in the south of Syria around Deraa. The Supreme Military Command (the U.S.-backed leadership of the FSA) has named him the commander of the Southern Front. He is the only member of these groups who has not expressed a wish to see an Islamist Syria.

ENDNOTES - APPENDIX

1. Thomas Joscelyn, "Al Qaeda and the threat in North Africa," *The Long War Journal*, November 21, 2013, *www.longwarjournal.org/archives/2013/11/al_qaeda_and_the_thr_1.php#ixzz2lPh2AfWc*.

2. *Ibid.*

3. *Ibid.*

4. See *www.washingtontimes.com/news/2013/dec/30/intel-com munity-still-insists-on-al-qaeda-ties-in-/#ixzz2pAozowT5.*

5. "Al Qaeda in the Islamic Magreb (AQIM)," New York: Council on Foreign Relations, available *www.cfr.org/terrorist-organizations-and-networks/al-qaeda-islamic-maghreb-aqim/p12717.*

6. See *www.longwarjournal.org/threat-matrix/archives/2013/07/a _new_ansar_al_sharia_in_the_s.php.*

7. See *www.brookings.edu/blogs/brookings-now/posts/2013/09/al-shabaab-somalia-terrorist-nairobi-mall-attack#.*

8. See *henryjacksonsociety.org/wp-content/uploads/2013/02/ Al-Qaeda-in-the-USAbridged-version-LOWRES-Final.pdf.*

9. See *www.ui.se/eng/upl/files/86861.pdf.*

10. Interview with Joshua Landis.

11. See *www.ui.se/eng/upl/files/86861.pdf.*

12. See *www.reasonedcomments.org/2014/01/010901-syria-war. html#.Utw9FtLn-9I.*

13. *Ibid.*

14. See *www.globalresearch.ca/syria-the-army-of-islam-saudi-arabias-greatest-export/5352638.*

15. See *www.longwarjournal.org/archives/2013/11/abdullah_ azzam_briga_1.php#ixzz2lDdwGiZn.*

16. See *www.joshualandis.com/blog/biggest-powerful-militia-leaders-syria/.*

17. See *www.joshualandis.com/blog/.*